MOTOR MAYHEM

MONSTER TRUCKS

KENNY ABDO

Fly!
An Imprint of Abdo Zoom
abdobooks.com

abdobooks.com

Published by Abdo Zoom, a division of ABDO, P.O. Box 398166, Minneapolis, Minnesota 55439. Copyright © 2024 by Abdo Consulting Group, Inc. International copyrights reserved in all countries. No part of this book may be reproduced in any form without written permission from the publisher. Fly!™ is a trademark and logo of Abdo Zoom.

Printed in the United States of America, North Mankato, Minnesota.
052023
092023

THIS BOOK CONTAINS RECYCLED MATERIALS

Photo Credits: Alamy, Getty Images, Shutterstock
Production Contributors: Kenny Abdo, Jennie Forsberg, Grace Hansen
Design Contributors: Candice Keimig, Neil Klinepier

Library of Congress Control Number: 2022946930

Publisher's Cataloging-in-Publication Data

Names: Abdo, Kenny, author.
Title: Monster Trucks / by Kenny Abdo
Description: Minneapolis, Minnesota : Abdo Zoom, 2024 | Series: Motor mayhem | Includes online resources and index.
Identifiers: ISBN 9781098281458 (lib. bdg.) | ISBN 9781098282158 (ebook) | ISBN 9781098282509 (Read-to-me ebook)
Subjects: LCSH: Truck racing--Juvenile literature. | Vehicles--Juvenile literature. | Monster trucks--Juvenile literature.
Classification: DDC 796.72--dc23

TABLE OF CONTENTS

MONSTER TRUCKS

With their supersized wheels and grisly-sounding engines, monster trucks crush all other **motorsports**!

Since the 1970s, monster trucks have raced, performed tricks, and crushed many unfortunate **foes**, delighting fans around the world!

PEED WORLD

START YOUR ENGINES

Souped-up pickup trucks became popular in the 1970s. They were used in tractor pulling and **mud bogging**.

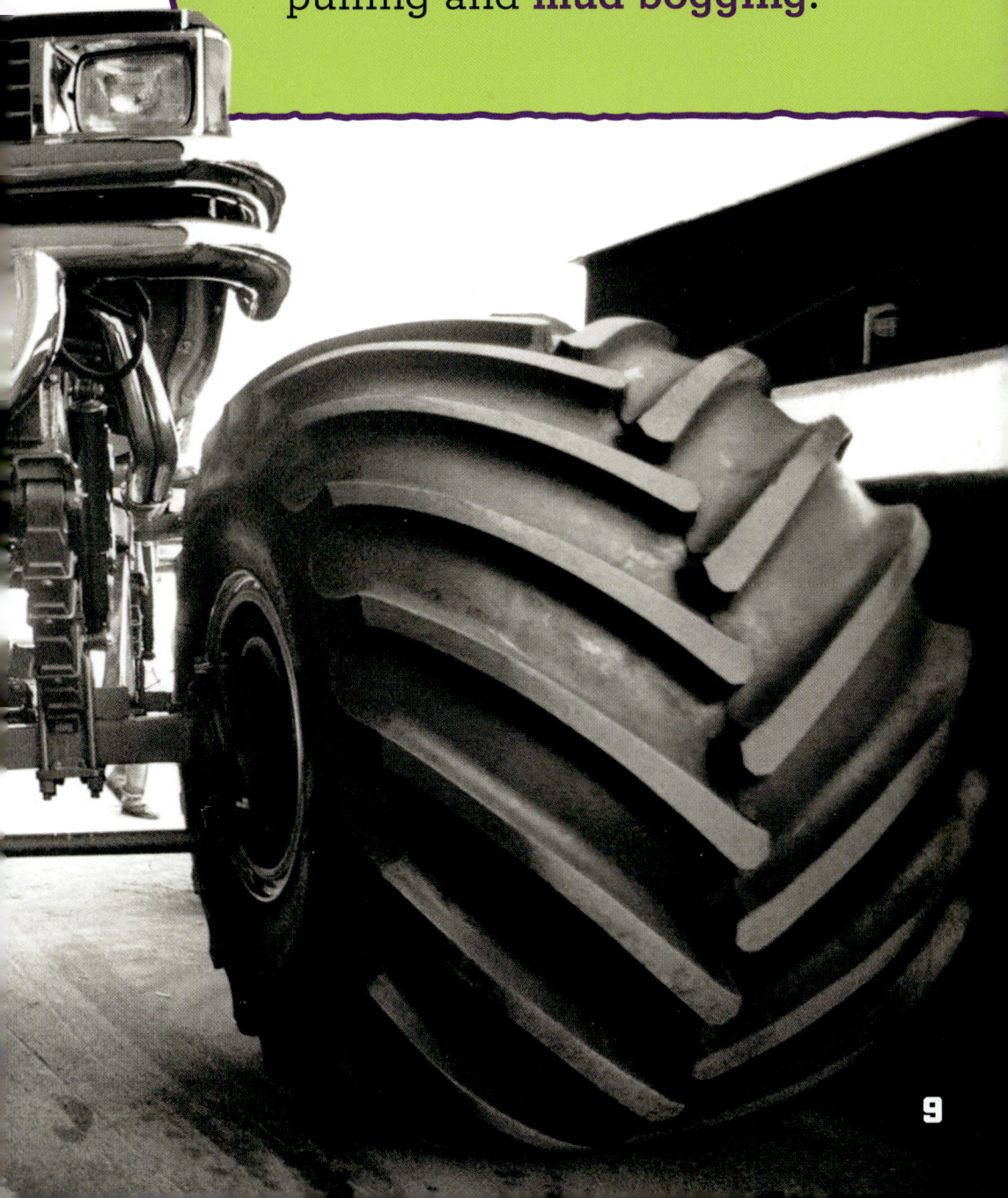

Bob Chandler **modified** his pickup truck with the biggest wheels and **axels** he could find. His iconic truck, Big Foot, caught national attention. Chandler became known as the father of monster trucks.

MAYHEM

Monster trucks are all custom built from **fiberglass**. The trucks may look intimidating, but they are very safe. Drivers also wear safety gear from head-to-toe.

A monster truck is more than 10 ft (3.04 m) tall and can weigh more than 10,000 lbs (4,535.9 kg). The tires alone are taller than most people.

There are many types of monster truck rallies. The most popular is Monster Jam. The first event was held in 1992 at the Silverdome in Pontiac, Michigan.

More than four million people attend Monster Jam events around the world every year.

There are three types of competition: **Freestyle**, Racing, and Two-Wheel skills.

BURNOUT

Monster trucks have been thrilling people for decades. Whether destroying other cars or performing **freestyle** stunts, audiences remain to be monster fans!

GLOSSARY

axel – the rod that connects and rotates the wheels while supporting the car's weight.

fiberglass – a material made of plastic and very fine fibers of glass.

foe – an opponent or rival.

freestyle – an extreme sport centered on stunt riding.

modification – an alteration or other result of modifying.

motorsport – a sport involving the racing of motor vehicles, like cars and motorcycles.

mud bogging – a type of off-road racing when a vehicle drives through a muddy track or pit.

souped-up – enhanced or increased in appeal, power, performance, or intensity.

ONLINE RESOURCES

Booklinks
NONFICTION NETWORK
FREE! ONLINE NONFICTION RESOURCES

To learn more about monster trucks, please visit **abdobooklinks.com** or scan this QR code. These links are routinely monitored and updated to provide the most current information available.

INDEX